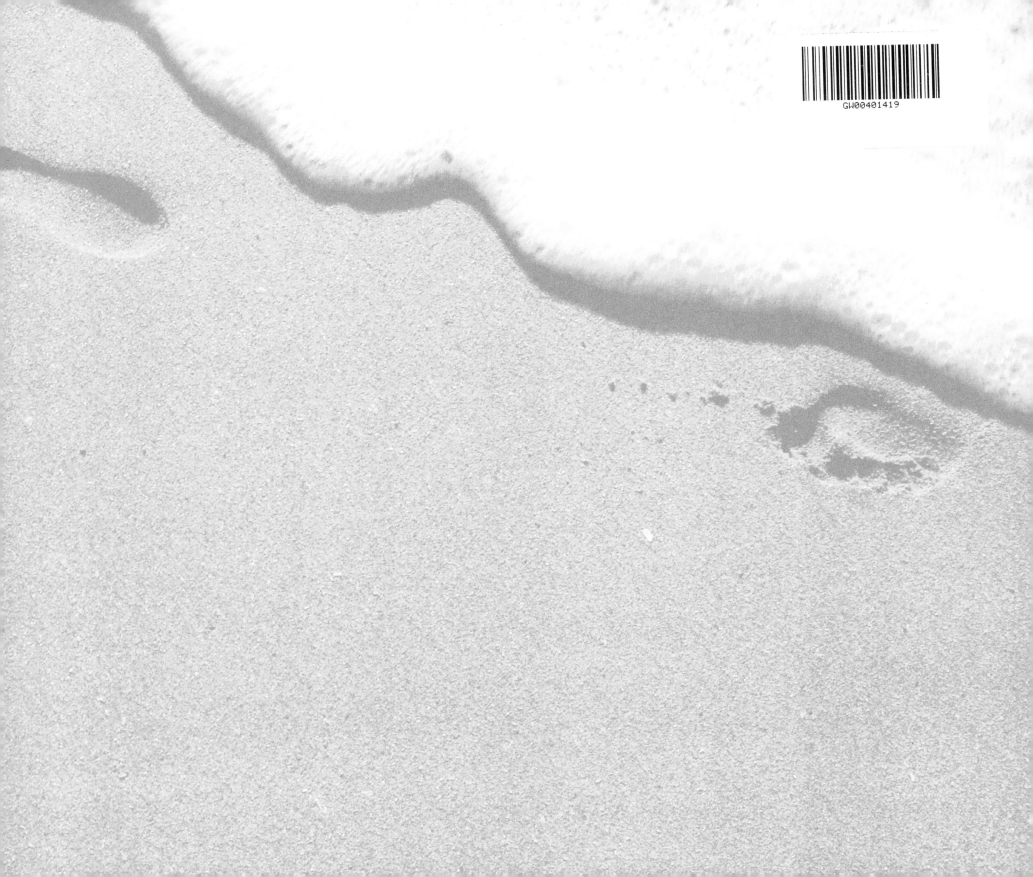

# BEACHES, BAYS AND COVES
## OF SYDNEY

First published in Australia in 2006 by
New Holland Publishers (Australia) Pty Ltd
Sydney • Auckland • London • Cape Town
14 Aquatic Drive Frenchs Forest NSW 2086 Australia
218 Lake Road Northcote Auckland New Zealand
86 Edgware Road London W2 2EA United Kingdom
80 McKenzie Street Cape Town 8001 South Africa

National Library of Australia Cataloguing-in-Publication Data:
Strewe, Oliver, 1950- .
Beaches, bays and coves of Sydney.
ISBN 1 74110 364 9.
1. Beaches - New South Wales - Sydney - Pictorial works.  2.
Bays - New South Wales - Sydney - Pictorial works.  3.
Inlets - New South Wales - Sydney - Pictorial works.  4.
Sydney Harbour (N.S.W.) - Pictorial works.  I. Title.

551.457099441

Publisher: Fiona Schultz
Managing Editor: Martin Ford
Project Editor: Lliane Clarke
Designer: Greg Lamont
Production Manager: Linda Bottari
Printer: Everbest, China

10 9 8 7 6 5 4 3 2 1

Front Cover: Coogee Beach
Back Cover: Turimetta Beach

# BEACHES, BAYS AND COVES OF SYDNEY

Oliver Strewe

NEW HOLLAND

# Contents

# Introduction

From above, Sydney's coastline looks like someone has shut their eyes, taken a pen and squiggled a line across a piece of paper—up and down and along, backwards and forwards, creating strangely shaped branches with gnarls, knobs and long snaky fingers. On the ground, those twists and turns translate into 350 kilometres of coastline, forming Sydney's six harbours and its innumerable beaches, bays and coves.

I was born in New Zealand and came to Sydney when I was 23. I'd been living in London, and my father, Odo, was living in Coogee. He had written many long letters to me full of enthusiasm about the beach and Australian beach culture. When I arrived in Sydney he was living in Bondi and I moved in with him there. I noticed the beautiful sharp light, the smell of frangipani, the red brick everywhere—and I went swimming or bodysurfing every day. The water wasn't always clean—old George Carpenter, a Jewish cockney Londoner who migrated to Sydney in 1919, said he'd never swim at Bondi—and some days there would be a strong waft of sewerage. But the beach was still fabulous and I've always come back to Bondi.

I lived for a while on beachfront Campbell Parade, when apartments were rackety and cheap to rent. There were always surfboards stored under the stairwell and sand on the foyer floor. My partner, Tina, and I had two children who had their first swims in the Bondi surf at about eight weeks old. From swimming or bodysurfing wherever I liked, I found myself at the north end of the beach, by the children's pool, where the kids splashed around in the shallow water and grownups sat on the sand and took turns buying cappucino from Speedo's cafe up the road (as far as I know, the first Sydney cafe to hit on the concept of 'babycino' for kids).

As my children grew up we moved along the beach. They learnt to swim in the calmer water between the flags at the north end, then caught waves bodysurfing or on boogie boards between the flags in the middle of the beach. Then they got their first 'foamies' and, eventually, their own surfboards:

they now surfed at the south end of the beach while I, exiled to the carpark, kept an eye on them through binoculars. It's a great cycle of life: like the rhythm of waves slapping onto sand there's the rhythm of years passing and families growing up, moving north to south along the beach and the whole thing starting again.

Until I become a grandparent, and return to the north end with my grandchildren, I have been restored to independent adulthood, swimming and bodysurfing wherever I like. And in this moment of rediscovered freedom, I decided to depart from the familiar and explore the beaches beyond this one where I live.

———————

The peculiar, complex shape of Sydney's coast is the result of its ancient geology. In his book *The Birth of Sydney,* Tim Flannery explains that about 230 million years ago the continent of Australia was still connected to Antarctica, both part of the supercontinent Gondwana, and the Sydney area was hundreds of kilometres inland, in a vast swampy valley. It was as far from the sea as Broken Hill is today. A great river flowed north from Antarctica, along what is now Australia's east coast, bringing with it grains of sand which, as the strength of its flow diminished, it deposited in what became the Sydney area. The sediments of sand, silt and clay from this and later rivers accumulated on flood plains and deltas in layers, burying the swamps and eventually filling the Sydney basin. The sand became cemented into sandstone and the finer silts and clays into shale and mudstone to a depth of about six kilometres. It's on this rocky foundation that Sydney was built.

About 190 million years ago, Gondwana began to split apart. One by one the continents broke away, with Australia and Antarctica the last to separate, about 40 million years ago. The separation of continents involves a process called rifting: heat from deep within the earth boils up along the line of the rift, causing a narrow bulge in the land. Then the bulge collapses at its centre, and a series of vast rocky steps is formed leading down to a central valley. Eventually the land on either side of this valley pulls apart and it is filled by the sea.

This process of bulging and collapse, Flannery says, changed the direction in which the rivers of the area flowed (from west to east) and 'cracked the sandstone in ways that dictated the position of harbours, coves, ridges and creeks. In essence, it laid Sydney out on a primitive, natural grid system that was profoundly to affect the city's development.'

Much of Sydney's sandstone is etched with ripple marks, showing in which direction ancient rivers flowed. It's also marked with a series of hairline fissures. These run in two directions, one parallel to the coast and the other perpindicular: this pattern, repeated on a much vaster scale, is that of the cracks that have guided the flow of rivers and creeks in the Sydney basin. Tim Flannery again: 'The watercourses that followed such cracks eventually dug the harbour and its tributaries, giving the waterway the complexity that even twentieth-century development is forced to follow.'

The result is a city uniquely connected to the coast: one view is that Sydney's six harbours (Pittwater, Middle and North Harbours, Port Jackson, Botany Bay and Port Hacking) and over 60 kilometres of surfing beaches allow more people to live, work and play close to the sea than in any other city in the world. And despite the the best efforts of developers, to some extent the city's coast is unassailable: it's kept that way by Sydney sandstone, a hard rock that tends to break away in big blocks, creating the vertical cliffs that are so characteristic of Sydney's coastline and so difficult to do anything with except admire.

---

Sydneysiders are defined by their love of the beach. Many only know their local beach or the one they grew up with; they seldom venture further afield. A friend who grew up in Watsons Bay went to the Watsons Bay baths as a small child, with occasional family outings to Parsley Bay and Neilson Park. As a teenager, he caught the bus to Bondi and, as he got older, to Bondi and Tamarama. He visited Coogee for the first time when he was 20. Now, the father of two young daughters, he goes mainly to Bronte. He's been to Manly a few times, but no more—exploring other beaches, he says, is 'a very rare event.' Such stories are common. 'Those who live in the eastern suburbs rarely venture beyond the CBD if they can help it. Those from the northern beaches think they have found nirvana, the North Shore knows it has', wrote a *Sydney Morning Herald* journalist at the time of the riots at Cronulla beach in 2005, in a one of series of articles examining Sydney's 'tribalism'.

Our favourite beach has all the advantages of familiarity: we know how to get there, where to park the car, where and when to swim, whether to surf or snorkel, whether it's best in a northerly, westerly or a sou'easter, when to stay away because it's too crowded or the tide's not right, where to buy an ice cream, a schooner of beer or a decent coffee. And it has none of the disadvantages: unusually, familiarity mostly doesn't breed contempt. There's no point in urging people from the southern side of the city to give the northern beaches a go, or vice versa, and probably no good reason to—it would only add to the clog of traffic on the roads. As my friend says, 'It's not as if you need to go to a different beach so you can have a different experience—once you know a beach well, it's different every time you go there.'

---

But exploring beyond local beaches can be a revelation. Freshwater, Chowder Bay, Milk Beach, the peninsula beaches (Newport, Avalon, Whale Beach, Palm Beach)—all these and many more were discoveries for me. So was Manly, with its surf beaches and still, protected coves—so much to choose from within such a small radius. And Collins Beach, also in the north, where I climbed down a steep set of steps to a rock platform and found myself in an other-world environment, standing at the edge of a deepwater cove thickly rimmed by forest, the stillness disturbed only by the mechanical thuds of the passing Manly ferry. At Balmoral I sat at the café and looked past the leafy branches of ancient figtrees, through to sparkling water.

Botany Bay held the biggest surprises. I began at Frenchman's Bay, and from there could see a strip of sand, a long way around by foot, too far to walk. So I drove around and found myself at Yarra Bay: the Palm Beach of the south, as a local called it when I signed in at the yacht club and settled myself out on the balcony, overlooking white sand with the sea just metres away. It's the only place in Sydney where you can watch the sun set over the water while drinking a beer at family prices, he said with pride. I said

I'd be back and I have been—there's room for everyone, people ride horses along the beach and the swimming couldn't be safer.

Another day I set off from the carpark at Voodoo Point, at Kurnell. I walked south for about 20 minutes, following a gently uphill route alongside sand dunes and a rusting sewage pipe, at one point startling a black snake that slithered away into the undergrowth. For much of the time I couldn't see the sea, tussocky dunes were in the way—then suddenly there below me was an exquisite little bay, almost circular, with white sand and water you can see straight through to the bottom of, sheltered from the wind. This is Boat Harbour, another beach that takes you back in time. There's a collection of small wooden shacks here, built sometime around the late 1930s and nothing else—imagine being one of the families lucky enough to spend a summer in one of these, days drifting by with nothing to do except swim and snorkel and play on the sand. Round the point from Boat Harbour is the long curve of beach that begins with Green Hills—a popular destination for four-wheel drivers—and stretches all the way to South Cronulla.

Elsewhere my discoveries were less dramatic but just as pleasing. I found a superb view of the start of the Sydney to Hobart yacht race from Washaway Beach at Balgowlah Heights, which looks straight out between North and South Heads. Edged by dramatic sandstone outcrops and native vegetation, this little fingernail of a beach (at high tide, there's hardly anything of it) has a wonderful shorebreak; one day when I was there the sea was what surfers dream of: glassy, with a regular, perfect swell.

Washaway is a designated nudist beach, unlike Little Congwong at the entrance to Botany Bay, where people go nude anyway. At Little Congwong I had a sharp exchange with a naked man who acted as if he was mayor of the beach: 'You're not allowed to take photographs here—it's illegal,' he told me imperiously. It was hard to resist pointing out that according to the nearby sign what actually was forbidden was taking off all your clothes, but I did. With the help of my friends—who in a gesture of peace generously took all their clothes off to go swimming—the situation was eventually smoothed over. I later spoke to a man who'd been fishing at Botany Bay for many years and often hauled up his net at Little Congwong, while nude men stood around and watched. 'You get all sorts here,' he said. 'Lumpy, stumpy and bumpy.'

Some places are attractive simply because they are there—Lady Martin's Beach at Point Piper and Kutti Beach in Vaucluse, for instance. Lady Martin's is reached down a long alleyway, Kutti Beach down an ankle-turningly steep and narrow flight of steps, concealed behind a gate at the side of the Vaucluse Amateur 12 Foot Sailing Club. Kutti is small beach, pretty but unspectacular; it's the fact of finding it there that's special—picking your way down dark, damp steps to a little moment of a beach, is like stepping through CS Lewis's wardrobe into another land, unexpected and remarkable.

These beaches are a reminder of the egalitarianism by which Australians still identify themselves. The real thing is harder and harder to find these days, but here's a remnant of it: mansions edge the sand and although their residents might wish general access to the beach was not just obscure but impossible, it doesn't matter—wealth carries no privilege here, the beach is for everyone to share.

Each Sydney beach has its own specific personality and its own culture. Take, for example, sand. Sand that's sparkling white is quartz grains coated with extra silica deposit; sand that's dull white is either worn quartz or limestone. Creamy-coloured sand is more than 90 per cent quartz. Sand that's yellow or gold or light brown is composed of impure quartz, feldspar and coloured shell. Grey sand has higher concentrations of volcanic or darker sedimentary rock, such as shale, in it.

Then there's the light. How the sea looks is all down to the light—whether it's summer light or winter, brilliant sunlight or overcast, morning light or dusk. As a general rule morning light is the best time—like at Manly, when the sun's already been up for an hour and the light is bouncing off the water, as if a silver blanket has been laid out across the whole bay.

Before the dawn, when there's just the slightest touch of light on the horizon, is my favourite time. During the day my eyes get distracted by everything else I can see. Before dawn the physical shape of a bay is most clearly revealed. I saw Congwong Bay like this very early one morning, reduced in the dimness to a single dark outline, and realised it was a completely different shape to the one I'd thought it was by day. I like to sit in the quiet dark and wait for the day to begin—if there's some wind making the sea a bit choppy the light dances over the bay, edging each little fragment of broken water with a rim of silver, orange or gold. Fog is good too. I photographed in the fog at Mackenzies Bay and it was beautiful: the fog kept shifting, thinning and thickening, and its moisture beaded on my face and in my hair.

---

The beaches, bays and coves of Sydney tell the city's history. Pristine Resolute Bay in the north, surrounded by the bush of Ku-ring-gai Chase National Park and accessible only by foot or by boat, is a reminder of the pre-European era. It's quiet there, except for birdsong, and sheltered from the wind. For Indigenous people this area was one of abundant resources—ready shelter and plenty of fresh fish, meat, fruit and other bush foods—described by historians as a prehistoric supermarket.

At the other end of history's spectrum is The Suction in Botany Bay, once an industrial site and now a place of old pipes, cracked cement and graffiti, where teenagers leap joyfully off a crumbling concrete wall into the sea below. Here the view is of cranes, oil refineries, the container port and the city skyline, and the rocks on the foreshore are old chunks and blocks of cement, their edges and corners being gradually worn away by the sea. Then there is Bronte Beach, where the narrow cutting that runs up to the road from the beach is lined with enormous homes all jammed up to the perimeters of the available land, replacing most of the original modest seaside cottages and telling a contemporary tale of overdevelopment and complicit or impotent local councils.

In between is the rest of Sydney's history: the Quarantine Station at North Head, first established in 1828, which for 140 years was used to accommodate newly arrived immigrants, initially in tents, in often miserable conditions. The gracious mansions of settler success stories (such as Strickland House at Milk Beach and Vaucluse House in Vaucluse). The cramped cottages at Watsons Bay, dating back to its early life as an isolated fishing village. The pavilions at Bondi and Manly and the kiosks at Balmoral and Neilson Park, which are ambitious, elegant responses to Sydney's nascent beach culture. Bondi Pavilion, built in 1928, contained dressing areas for 12 000 people, Turkish baths, shops and a ballroom. Then there is the shacks at Boat Harbour and elsewhere in Botany Bay—a reminder of the Aboriginal Mission at La

Perouse—and the desperate shelters made out of flattened kerosene tins, bits of driftwood and sacking, anything people could find, by families made homeless and destitute by the Depression of the 1930s, and of the struggle faced by many post-war migrants.

'{Dad} had found a little shack at Yarra Bay for us to live in—on Hill no 60—that was the address,' wrote one migrant of her arrival here as a child in the early 1950s. 'As children we loved living there—it was such fun to be able to swim, fish and picnic as we liked. But it must have been hard for mum. There was no electricity and only one water tap to service everyone living in that community at Yarra Bay.'

---

Many of Sydney's placenames come from its first coastal inhabitants—the Carigal, Cadigal, Makeygal, Muru-ora-dlal and others, known collectively as Eora—such as Bondi (from boondi, or bundi, meaning 'noise of water breaking over rocks), Cronulla (from kurranulla, 'place of pink seashells'), and Coogee (from koojah, 'a stinking place').

Manly was named by Governor Phillip in recognition of the noble, 'manly' bearing of the local Aborigines he encountered there. Port Hacking was named by Matthew Flinders after a ship's pilot, Henry Hacking. The name Botany Bay recognises 'The great quantity of plants Mr Banks and Dr Solander found in this place', according to an entry in James Cook's diary. Pittwater was once Pitt Water, declared by Captain Arthur Phillip to be 'the finest piece of water I ever saw' and named after the then English Prime Minister, William Pitt the Younger.

Frenchman's Bay was named after explorer Comte de la Perouse, whose ships sailed into Botany Bay just six days after the First Fleet. La Perouse never met First Fleet commander Captain Arthur Phillip, but (according to *Ruth Park's Sydney*) Phillip's men visited the French ships and enjoyed French hospitality, including fish from Botany Bay: in one day, Ruth Park reports, the French sailors caught nearly 2000 snapper.

Journeying the beaches, bays and coves of Sydney has taught me a new respect for the history of Sydney's sewage system. Once upon a time, everything went into the water: sewage, grease, waste from factories. Sydney's first sewers, laid in the 1850s, drained raw sewage into the harbour off Bennelong Point, where the Opera House is now. The idea was the ocean current would deal with it all. It's a view from the past but not yet consigned to history—at Malabar I met a fisherman, Brian, who'd fished there all his life. He told me that one day in the 1960s he was coming home in his boat from a day's fishing and when he entered the bay bream and whiting were jumping out of the water. But those fish don't normally jump, he said. The next morning the beach and the rocks were littered with dead fish. The official explanation was that they'd been dumped there by a passing trawler. But everyone knew they'd died because of chemical waste discharged into the sea. He told me of another time when chemical waste turned the whole bay bright green.

There are now ten coastal sewage treatment plants in Sydney with the three largest, at Bondi, Malabar and North Head, responsible for treating most of the city's sewage. Up until the early 1990s these treatment plants discharged their load of waste through single pipe outfalls off rocky headlands into water less than 10 metres below the surface. Gradually, public outrage about the severe and often highly visible pollution of beaches near the outfalls had an effect. The decision was made to divert the effluent from the three sewage treatment plants to offshore deepwater outfalls, where it would be expelled into the sea through multi-port diffusers across a zone of between 500-750 metres at depths of 60-80 metres.

Some experts feel this is still not nearly good enough—technology is readily available to allow effluent to be treated to a much higher level before discharge—but for everyday beach users the difference has been considerable. Sea that smells of salt, not sewage. Catching fish (though whatever you do, don't eat them). The improvement is confirmed by the results of monitoring by the New South Wales state government's Beachwatch and Harbourwatch programs, established in 1989 and 1994 respectively. Both programs have found that more ocean and harbour beaches comply with water quality criteria more often than they used to, with 86 of the 129 sites assessed complying 100 per cent of the time in the summer 2003-4 (the latest at time of writing).

So the beaches are cleaner, which makes them more attractive. But 'attractive' isn't an objective term. People love 'their' beach, the one they know. They become part of its life, they identify with it and care for it. At its worst, that becomes the tribalism that creates insiders and outsiders, inclusion and exclusion. At its best, it's the community that results in surf lifesaving, nippers for the young children or loosely-formed swim clubs, in people doing things together (like the voluntary bushcare groups that are slowly transforming beaches such as Jibbon or Bronte and Tamarama) or on their own to look after their beach.

I've noticed a few other things. When people walk along the sand at the edge of the sea, they follow the path that the incoming waves lay out for them. The tracks they leave outline the shape of the sea on the sand. When they swim, the surf bundles them up, organising them into clusters. It's confirmation, if needed, that people never have the upper hand.

You can visit a beach five, ten times and each time find it uninviting—but when you're next there it may be that all the right elements are in place: it's high tide, there's no wind, the sun's shining, the surf is just the way you like it. Suddenly it's a magic place to be.

*Oliver Strewe*

*The Birth of Sydney*, edited and introduced by Tim Flannery. Text Publishing, Sydney, 1999. *Ruth Park's Sydney*, by Ruth Park. Duffy & Snellgrove, Sydney, 1999

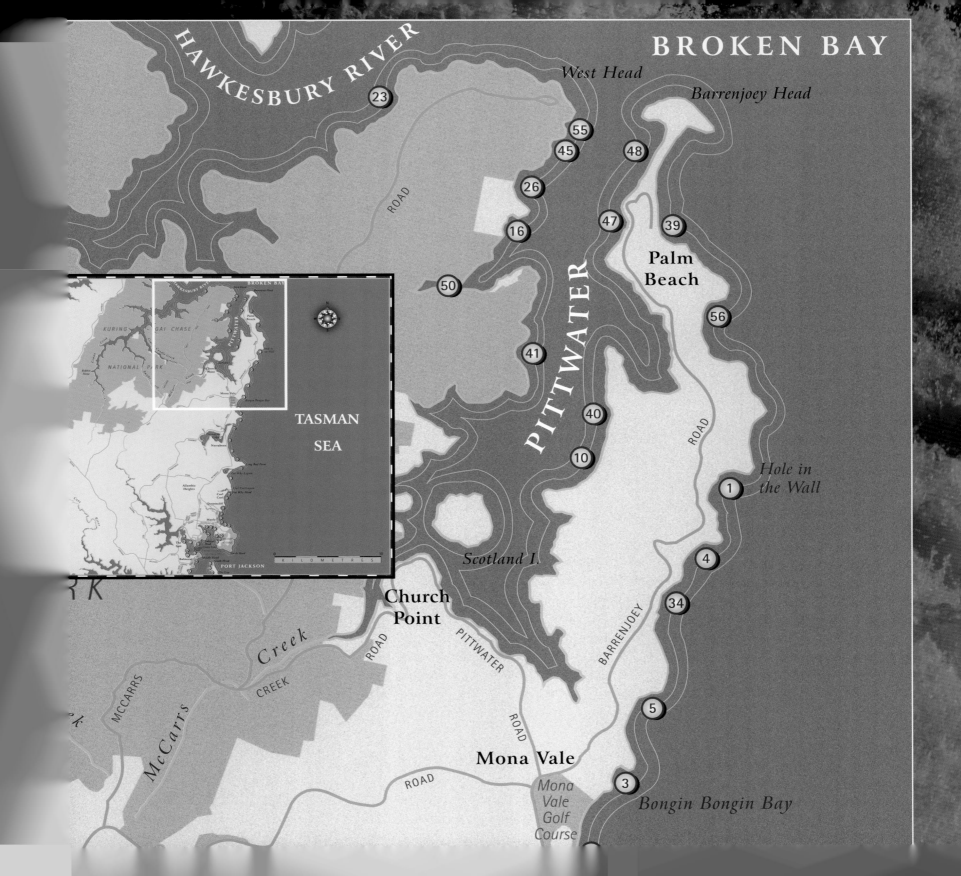

HAWKESBURY RIVER

BROKEN BAY

West Head

Barrenjoey Head

Palm
Beach

PITTWATER

Hole in
the Wall

Scotland I.

Church
Point

Creek

McCarrs

McCARRS

CREEK

ROAD

PITTWATER

ROAD

BARRENJOEY

ROAD

ROAD

Mona Vale

Mona
Vale
Golf
Course

Bongin Bongin Bay

ROAD

BROKEN BAY

HAWKESBURY RIVER

KURING GAI CHASE

NATIONAL PARK

PITTWATER

Palm
Beach

Church
Point

Mona Vale

TASMAN
SEA

PORT JACKSON

KILOMETRES

# Pittwater, Broken Bay and The Hawkesbury River

*left:* RESOLUTE BEACH *above:* CLAREVILLE BEACH

*above:* FLINT AND STEEL BEACH *right:* PORTUGUESE BEACH

PITTWATER, BROKEN BAY AND THE HAWKESBURY RIVER

*left:* WEST HEAD BEACH *above:* PARADISE BEACH

*left and above:* STATION BEACH

*left and above:* THE BASIN

*left:* SNAPPERMAN BEACH

*left:*
GREAT MACKERAL BEACH

*right:*
CURRAWONG BEACH

# Northern Beaches

PALM BEACH

WHALE BEACH

NORTHERN BEACHES

AVALON BEACH

AVALON BEACH

BILGOLA BEACH

NEWPORT BEACH

BUNGAN BEACH

NORTHERN BEACHES

BASIN BEACH

MONA VALE BEACH

WARRIEWOOD BEACH

NORTHERN BEACHES

TURIMETTA BEACH

NORTHERN BEACHES

NARRABEEN LAGOON

COLLAROY BEACH

FISHERMANS BEACH

*left:* LONG REEF BEACH *above:* FISHERMANS BEACH

DEE WHY BEACH

NORTH CURL CURL BEACH

*above:* FISHERMANS BEACH *right:* CURL CURL BEACH

*left:* FRESHWATER BEACH *above:* QUEENSCLIFF BEACH

MANLY BEACH

SHELLY BEACH

FAIRY BOWER BEACH

## Inset map (upper left)

BROKEN BAY

HAWKESBURY RIVER

West Head

Barrenjoey Head

Palm Beach

KURING - GAI CHASE

PITTWATER

NATIONAL PARK

Coaster Creek

Garland

Bobbin Head

Church Point

Mona Vale

Bungan Beach Bay

TASMAN
SEA

Narrabeen

Long Reef Point

Dee Why Head

Dee Why Lagoon

Allambie
Heights

Curl Curl

Dee Why Head

Queenscliff

Manly

Dobroyd Head

North Head

The Spit

Balmoral

Middle Head

South Head

PORT JACKSON

KILOMETRES

## Main map

WAY

SYDNEY

LAUDERDALE AVE

30

21  46

20   18   31

24

44

28   14

11                                    49        MILITARY
                                                  RESERVE

CUTLER

8      7         53        Dobroyd
The                                    Head        42
Spit
                                Grotto    Crater Cove
                                Point
                  19                    SYDNEY HARBOUR
                                        NATIONAL PARK        North Head
ROAD
                  2      12

MILITARY           Balmoral         RD       Middle Head
                                            South Head
                        38
                  MIDDLE                           PORT JACKSON
            BRADLEYS   HEAD
            HEAD              27
            RD                6

                  9          54       The Gap

# Middle Harbour and North Harbour

MIDDLE HARBOUR AND NORTH HARBOUR

*left:* QUARANTINE BEACH *above:* SPRING COVE

COLLINS BEACH

MIDDLE HARBOUR AND NORTH HARBOUR

LITTLE MANLY COVE

1209
1287
1300
1301
1238
1233
Tickled Pink
1209
RPAYC
Tickled Pink
MISCHIEF
RPAYC
1300

MANLY COVE

*above:* MANLY COVE *right:* DELWOOD BEACH

*above:* FAIRLIGHT BEACH *right:* FORTY BASKETS BEACH

MIDDLE HARBOUR AND NORTH HARBOUR

*above:* REEF BEACH *right:* WASHAWAY BEACH

*above:* CLONTARF BEACH *right:* CASTLE ROCK BEACH

MIDDLE HARBOUR AND NORTH HARBOUR

*above:* CHINAMAN'S BEACH *right:* COBBLERS BEACH

MIDDLE HARBOUR AND NORTH HARBOUR

BALMORAL BEACH

EDWARDS BEACH

MIDDLE HARBOUR AND NORTH HARBOUR

BALMORAL SWIMMING CLUB

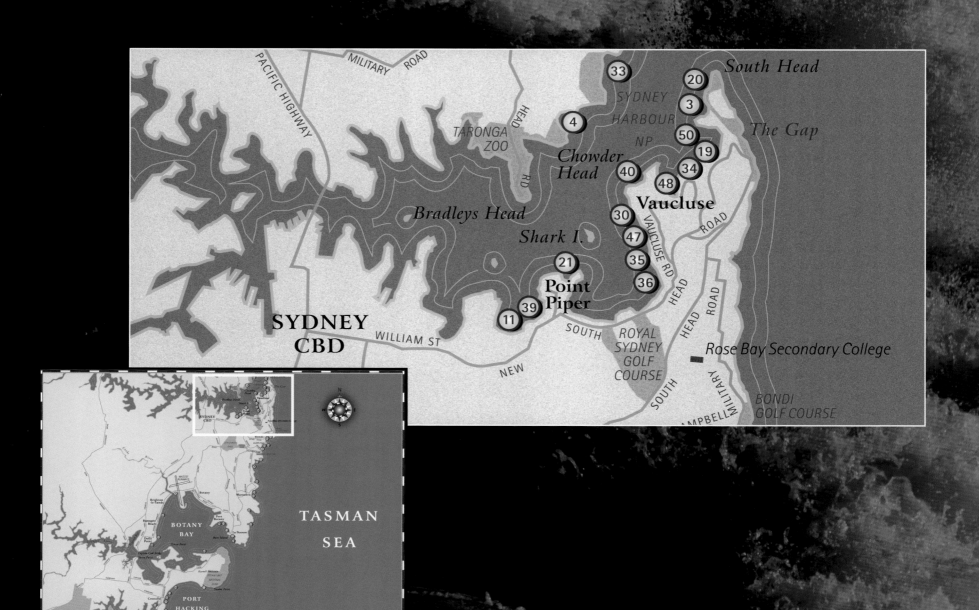

# Port Jackson

MILK BEACH

*above:* LADY BAY BEACH *right:* PARSLEY BAY

SHARK BAY

PORT JACKSON

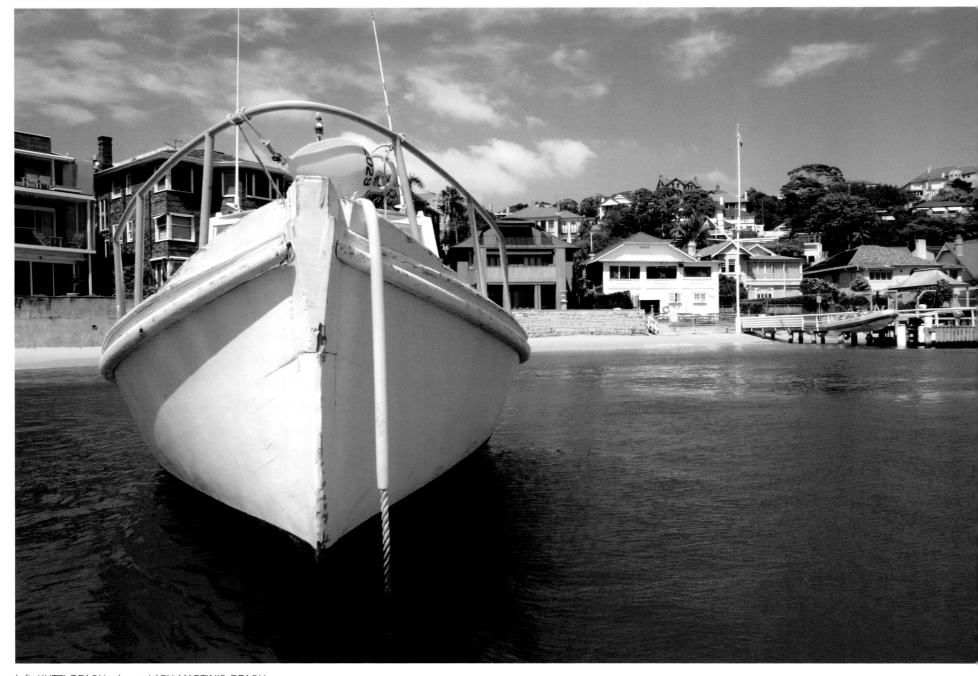

*left:* KUTTI BEACH *above:* LADY MARTIN'S BEACH

SEVEN SHILLINGS BEACH

PORT JACKSON

WATSONS BAY

CAMP COVE

*above:* VAUCLUSE BAY *top right:* DOUBLE BAY *right:* QUEENS BEACH

CHOWDER BAY

PORT JACKSON

OBELISK BEACH

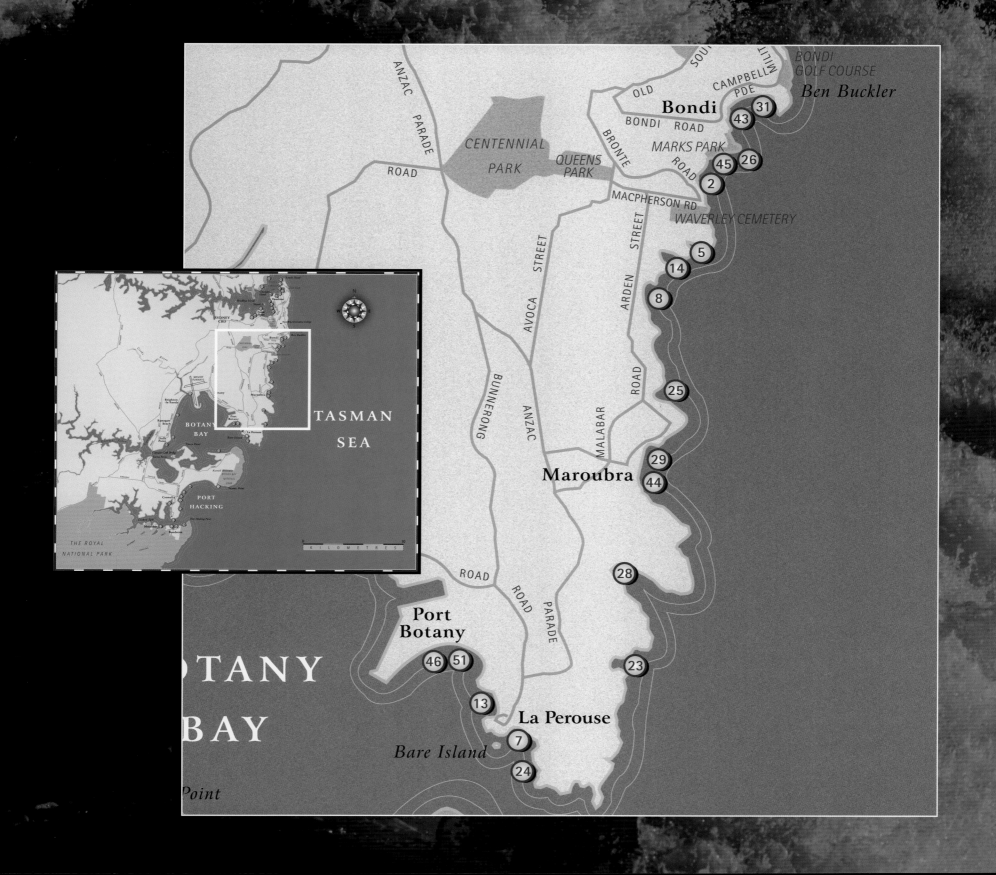

# City Surf Beaches

BONDI BEACH

CITY SURF BEACHES

BONDI BEACH

CITY SURF BEACHES

MACKENZIES BAY

CITY SURF BEACHES

TAMARAMA BEACH

CITY SURF BEACHES

BRONTE BEACH

BRONTE BEACH

CITY SURF BEACHES

CLOVELLY BEACH

CITY SURF BEACHES

COOGEE BEACH

*above:* GORDONS BAY *right:* LURLINE BAY

CITY SURF BEACHES

*left:* MAHON POOL *above:* MAROUBRA BEACH

MAROUBRA BEACH

MAROUBRA BEACH

CITY SURF BEACHES

LONG BAY, MALABAR

LONG BAY, MALABAR

CITY SURF BEACHES

LITTLE BAY

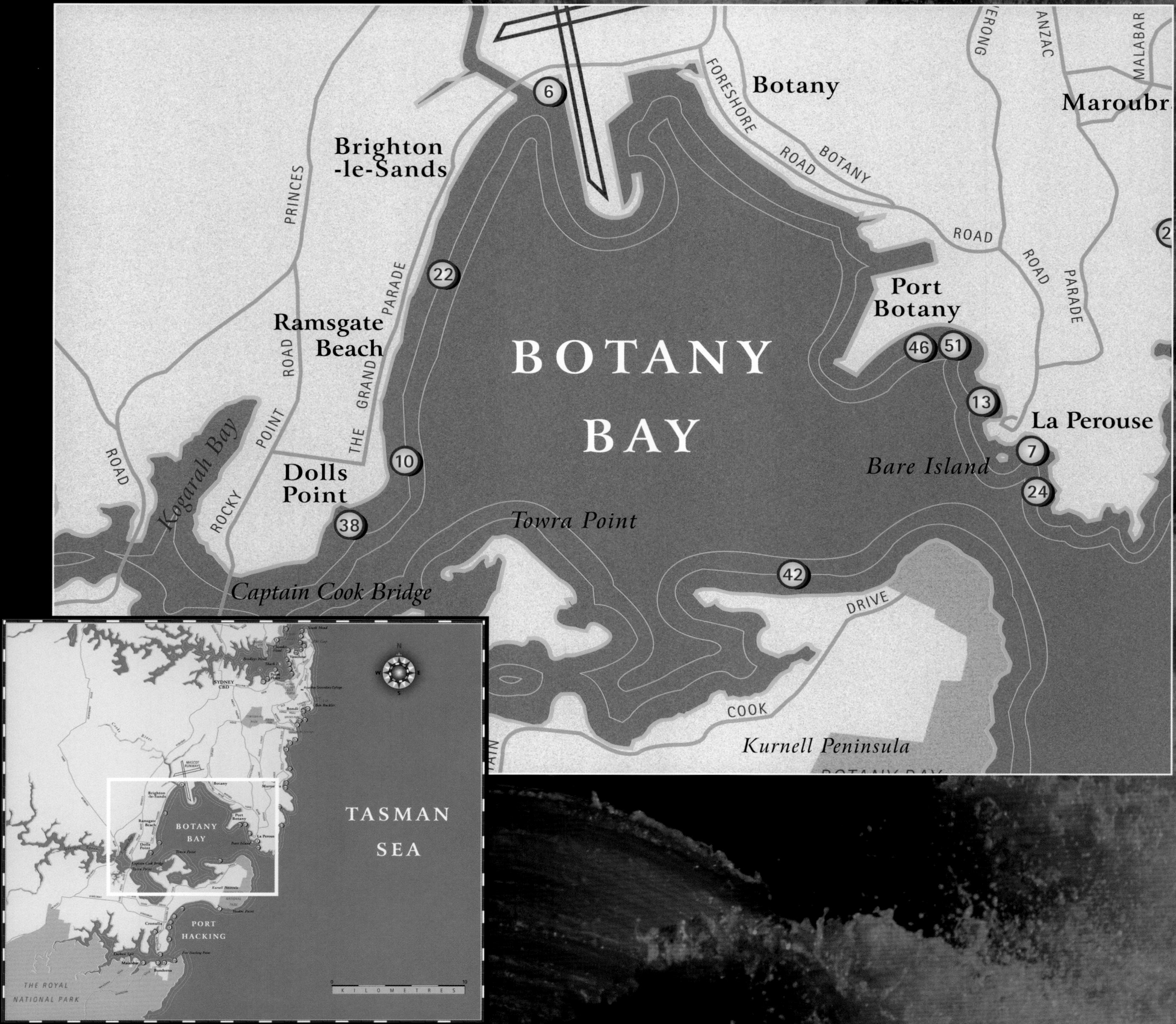

BOTANY BAY

Brighton -le-Sands

Botany

Maroubr[a]

Ramsgate Beach

Port Botany

Kogarah Bay

Dolls Point

La Perouse

Bare Island

Towra Point

Captain Cook Bridge

Kurnell Peninsula

TASMAN SEA

PORT HACKING

THE ROYAL NATIONAL PARK

KILOMETRES

# Botany Bay

BOTANY BAY

*left:* BOTANY BAY *above:* SILVER BEACH

*above:* LITTLE CONGWONG BEACH *right:* DOLLS POINT

BOTANY BAY

SANDRINGHAM BAY

BRIGHTON-LE-SANDS

*above:* LADY ROBINSONS BEACH *right:* FRENCHMAN'S BAY

BOTANY BAY

left: YARRA BAY above: THE SUCTION

*left:* CONGWONG BEACH *above:* COMMONWEALTH BEACH

ans die every year.

LADY ROBINSONS BEACH

*Kurnell Peninsula*

BOTANY BAY

NATIONAL

PARK

*Voodoo Point*

49

12

32

**Cronulla**

9

15

41

PORT

HACKING

*Port Hacking Point*

*Deeban Spit*

37

18

**Maianbar** 27

17 16

**Bundeena**

TASMAN

SEA

# Cronulla and Port Hacking

WANDA BEACH

CRONULLA AND PORT HACKING

BOAT HARBOUR

WANDA BEACH

GUNNAMATTA BAY

CRONULLA BEACH

CRONULLA AND PORT HACKING

NORTH CRONULLA BEACH

*left:* SALMON HAUL BAY *above:* GUNYAH BEACH

SIMPSONS BAY

*above and right:* JIBBON BEACH

CRONULLA AND PORT HACKING

*next page:* HORDERNS BEACH